Poems for My Valentine

(If only my heart could sing)

By Daphne Marie McDonald

<u>This book was written for all that love</u>

<u>To all of the lovers</u>

Keep love alive in your hearts

It is the only thing that keeps

Things from falling apart

ISBN:

978-1-105-40602-7

CHAPTER ONE

Love is Easy

Eternal Love

There is no hope

For my reprieve

In my heart

I will love you eternally

Love Is Like a Flower

Love is like a flower

That grows in the spring

When harsh weather comes

It doesn't die, just sleeps

And when the sky is bright

Its beauty comes shining through

That is the way love is when it is true!

My Gift to You

I cannot give you diamonds

Or a mansion on the hill

Cover you in silk garments

Even though it is my will

I only have my love to give

And the promise it will last

When the life of material things

Have long ago passed

Feelings

If you refuse to know pain

You refuse to know pleasure

You cannot feel one and not the other

All I have

I love you

With all my heart

Never deceitful

Or Selfish

Always honorably

Faithfully

That is how important your love is

To me, I love you

With every beat of my heart

With a love that will never

Part

A love that will never die

It is eternal, Everlasting

That is how real your love is

To me

I love you

With all that I hold dear

With every beat of this heart inside of me

That is how good your love is

And I vow never to leave

I have love

I have love and it is kind

And when I sing off key

Love doesn't mind

I have love

And it is sweet

And nothing can take love

Away from me

I have love and it is fine

And can only be compared

To

A rare bottle of wine

Natural Resources

The Lord's natural resource

Like the trees, lakes

Mountain and Streams

Love Approached

Precious and pure

That I had to share

With all the world

All that I have to give

Wondering

People wonder why I choose to

Love You

Why are you at the center of my heart?

People wonder why I choose to love you

And vow we will never part

It is because you soothe my mind

In these troubling times

It is because when we touch

Chills run down my spine

People wonder why I choose to

Love You

They will never understand why

My spirit longs for you when we are apart

And you are so important

To the beating of my heart

People wonder why I choose to

Love you

They can't see the way my heart smiles

For more than a minute or awhile

The Reward

True Love,

Looks not for a great reward

Medal

Or citation

It rejoices

Only in the fact

That the battle was won

And the casualties are none.

A Gift from Above

God smiled upon my life

Blessed me with you

I thank him for a love

That is true

Through the good times

And the bad

We can be secure

In our love

Our union was ordained

From God above

My True Love

My true love arrived and slowly but surely,

Brick by brick

He tore down the wall

I had built up over the years to protect

Myself from imposters

Like the ones I allowed access to my heart

In the past

Then you walked into my life

My true love

And I welcomed you across

The thresholds of my world

And you walked through the

Rooms in my mind and I

Revealed to you all my hopes and dreams

You performed open heart surgery

On my heart

And my heart healed

So I could love you

Something no one else could ever do!

Can You Keep a Secret?

Can you keep a secret?

If I whispered in your ear

How much I care for you

My Dear

Can you keep a secret?

If I told you of my dreams

That you will always be

Close to me

Can you keep a secret?

If I had it written in the sky

That you are the joy

Of my life

Can you keep a secret?

Just between me and you

That are love is

True

What a Mystery Love Can Be

What a mystery love can be

And love has come to me

What a gift love can be

Thank you love

For the present you gave to me

What a battle love can be

However,

We will not declare defeat

What a blessing love can be

God knew I needed THEE!

No Duplications

A love like ours cannot be duplicated

When we touch fireworks are created

When there were no words to say

There would be better days

Life without you would tear apart my soul

Together we are one

Together we are whole

The love that we share

Could be called unique

Because there is nothing more important to me

A love like ours can never be duplicated

When we kiss fireworks are created

CHAPTER TWO

Love Is Priceless

Imagining

Imagine how the world would be

If you weren't sharing my life next to me

Imagine if I had to live alone

And when I arrived you weren't home

Imagine if I opened my eyes

And you were no longer by my side

I am glad I don't need to

Imagine

Any of these things

And because of your love

My heart sings

Claim Love

Search no more

Wander not through the wilderness

Hide not among the trees

Claim Love

It is yours don't be intimidated

Don't be afraid,

Don't be worried love won't stay

Claim Love

It is yours don't cover your face

Don't seek shelter

And please don't hide'

Take the blinders off of your eyes

Claim Love

Before it slips away

<u>Our First Kiss</u>

Your lips touched mine

A feeling of ecstasy came over me

Made me thirst for more

Made me hunger for more

I long for the next time

Your lips touch mine!

<u>The Spy in Our Backyard</u>

This old oak

It seems has and will always be

A part of you and me

It spied kisses

Listened to wishes

Shared secret talks

Viewed endless walks

Caught my wedding bouquet

To the bridesmaids' dismay

This old oak

Shall always be an eternal part of you and me.

No Explanation

I don't owe the world an explanation

Concerning why I love you

No one can see how deep our love goes

Without an X-ray machine

I wake up every morning

Anticipating the sound of your voice

And the sound of your

Good Morning

No one would ever be able to see

How much you mean to me

And I need no explanation

They shouldn't expect me to explain

Can anyone explain away the rain?

That is how special

Our love is to me

It causes my heart to weep

Tears of happiness

Yes

This kind of love

Is too powerful to explain

And

I don't owe the world an explanation

For my joy

When I see your face

And the love that gets

Stronger

With each passing day

Your Kind

Your Kind is dangerous

Because I have become

Addicted to your loving

Your kind is faithful

Because I realize

How certain is your loving

Your kind could keep me

Wrapped around your finger forever

Influencing is your loving!

<u>Since Love Arrived</u>

Since love arrived my bed is warm

And I am so thankful for the

Warmth that covers me at night

Since love arrived

I have something to hold tight

Especially

In the middle of the night

When nightmares try to

Invade my life

Since love arrived

There is a great big smile on my face

And to others I may look

Like a clown

However, I am just happy to have

Love around

Since love arrived

My room is never silent

There are sounds of passion everywhere

How wonderful to know

That love cares

Since love arrived

Everything is full of light

All of the corners of my life

Are bright

All because love arrived

Took me for a ride

Then took its place

By my side

Natural Resources

A natural resource

Like the trees

Lakes

Mountains

And Streams

Love approached

Untarnished

Precious and Pure

That I had to share

With all the world

All that I had to give

Source of Happiness

You are the source of my happiness

You are the source of my joy

You are the source of my future

You walked into my world

You asked to show me how

Great love can be

So, you wrapped me in your love

And brought me serenity

You wanted in

And you weren't afraid

Do I deserve this love?

Maybe yes

Maybe No

However,

I will never let it go!

There You Stood

There you stood all alone

There I stood all alone

Will you meet me half way?

Will you reach out for me half way?

Your side my side

Becoming one

There you stood all alone

There I stood all alone

Will you meet me half way?

Love me half way

Touch me half way

My side your side

Becoming one

Relationships

All relationships have

Their spring and winter

I would say that we are in our spring

Everything is new

And I am crazed

Over you

Everything about our love is alive

Growing and thriving

We are discovering the best of you and me

We will store up some of this love

For other times

When winter comes knocking on our door

And we may need some of this

Happiness we have stored away

In our hearts

And remembering how

Good our love can be when it isn't

In deep freeze

Eyes of Love

There are times we don't see eye to eye

It seems as if we never agree

There is still one thing that will always

Ring true

You love me and I love you!

Just For You

My Love is just for you

And for you only

My heart is beating

Just For You

My thoughts and dreams

For the future are

Just For You

And I long to be loved

Kissed and hugged

My loving and longing

Are

Just For You

Childhood Dreams

When I was a child

I would dream about how love would be

For me

I believed God created someone just for me

That they would find me in this world

Of hearts that number in the billions

And you were there

And were destined to meet

You found me

Took me in your arms

And promised to cause my

Heart no harm

You were there holding my hand

As we walked through the sand

And I am grateful

That my dreams came true

And god blessed

This thankful heart

With loving

You

That Special Place

There is a place

Where peace is peaceful

And

Rest is restful

Joy is joyful

Where every is everything

And

Happy is happily

Hope is hopeful

Time is timeless

There is a place

Where heaven is heavenly

And eternal is eternally

There is a place

Where love is lovely

And that place is in your heart

Time and Time Again

Time and time again

You have touched my heart

Touched my soul

Time and time again

I will remind you that I love you

I need love

And that you will always be mine

Time and time again

You make me smile

Make me laugh

And make me happy that you are in

My life

Time and time again

I will kiss you

I will caress you

And want you in my life, Time and time again

Steps

If you take one step

I will take two

If you kissed me once

I would kiss you twice

If you hold me close

I would hold you near

If you yelled to me

"I Love You"

I would shout

"I feel the same way too"

If you vow to never leave

I will promise to love you

Through out

Eternity

Remember my love

If you take one step

I will take two

Determined to allow nothing

To come between me and you

Because Of You

I was apprehensive didn't want to give

Love

Another try

And then you awaken

My spirit from the dead

You lead me down a corridor

Filled with promises

Hopes and dreams

I didn't know if I should hide

Runaway or scream

For

I was apprehensive didn't want to give

Relationship

Another try

Then you kissed away my tears

And told me not to be afraid

That you would take special

Care of my heart

And never leave me alone

Filled To the Rim

I am filled to the rim of my heart

With your love

So much so, it resembles a flood

I fell like the luckiest

Person on Earth

Because you agreed

To share my life

Every corner of my mind

Is filled with thoughts

Of you

Dreams of you

There isn't a moment

Those thoughts of you

Don't cross my mind

All of these feelings

Can only be understood

By those in love

And they know what I mean

When I say my heart is filled

To the rim with your love

My Favorite Word

Love

A Beautiful word to my ears

Love

Is what I offer you my Dear.

Love

Is what I want in our Life.

Love

Has brought us together

For life

ALL I HAVE

I love you,

With all my heart

Never deceitfully

Or selfishly

Always honorably

Faithfully

My love for you is pure

A Message from the Author

To the great Architect of Love

My Lord and Savior Jesus Christ

That inspired me to write this book

I hope this work of prose is a

Blessing to your Life

And to the one you love

Please share with others

In the hope that

They can be blessed by

Words that describes

God's greatest gift to the human spirit

www.ingramcontent.com/pod-product-compliance
Ingram Content Group UK Ltd.
Pitfield, Milton Keynes, MK11 3LW, UK
UKHW041905190726
13854UKWH00003B/1103